ECHOES OF ECHAD

SETTING AND PREPARING WAY FOR THE NEXT GENERATION
THROUGH KEY REVELATIONS OF SUCCESS

Naomie Praise Kabasele

Library of Congress Control Number	2021909161
Paperback:	978-1-8382737-2-9
eBook:	978-1-8382737-3-6

United Kingdom

First things first...

Welcome unity at the slightest
opportunity.

Unity is about togetherness.
First be together with yourself.

Believe in yourself, walk
together with yourself.

Embrace unity in your heart.
Be in unity with your mind in
order to prosper.

Be united with yourself then
you can unite with others.

When you unite with others, it
shows you have responsibilities
with them.

Unity is like building a house because you will need different pieces for it to come together.

Unity can protect and covers the exposed.

hen unity is around, everyone is happy.

Unity embraces the vulnerable and lonely people.

Unity is a friend of peace and joy.

Unity is a friend of God but an enemy of the devil.

Unity is supposed to smell sweet because it's unique.

Unity is meant to be pure.

Unity removes shame.
Unity brings relevance.

Unity knows equality and justice.

Unity knows no racism no discrimination or unfairness.

Unity comes from God.
Unity is God.

The Hebrew word for unity is
ECHAD,

Meaning one-ness in reference
to the nature and character of
God and to Man's relationship
to God.

Unity is trinity.
Unity is an element of
encouragements.

God brought unity to the world, that's why our sins were forgiven.

Jesus Christ was sent to the world, for humanity to reconcile with God himself.

This is called love and unity.

The beauty of Jesus Christ dying on the Cross brought humanity to unity.

Unity brings attraction.
You will be like a magnet that
people would want to always
stick around you.

Unity destroys bullying, arguments, guilt, anger, jealousy, hatred, slandering and gossip.

Around those fighting,
Be the one to bring
unity in the atmosphere.
Do this by good advice.

Unity is meant to be sincere.

Unity will cause you to hold your enemy's hand.

Unity will cause you to hug others with love.

Unity will cause you to love.

Unity will cause you to eat and drink together.

Unity will cause you to smile.

Unity causes communication and dialogue.

Unity causes people to pray and fast.

Unity leads to fulfilments of goals.

Unity will cause you to forgive and move on with your life.

Unity leads to focus and discipline.

Unity causes your mind to be positive.

Unity brings joy.

Unity brings friends together.

Unity brings families together.

Unity brings the governments together.

Unity brings leaders and churches together.

Unity brings discipline, value and respect.

Unity brings peace.

Unity will keep you away from toxic things and people.

Unity will teach you more about yourself and others.

Unity is a product of success, establishment and elevation.

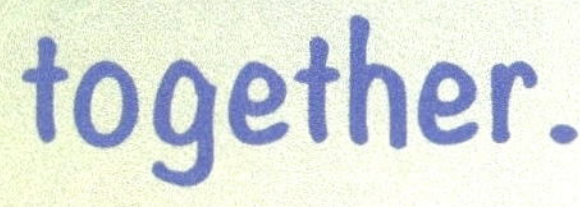

Unity brings nations together.

Unity brings businesses together.

Unity breaks the silence

Unity breaks chains.

In unity you can get things done.

Most importantly,
God is in support of unity
because he hates division.

As you promenade with friends
be in unity.

Unity shows holiness.

Unity shows your identity and purpose.

Unity brings kindness.

Unity allows people to share.

Unity allows people to listen.

Unity allows you to feel comfortable around others.

Unity can give you a good name.

Unity can make you famous
because everyone would want
to copy you.

Unity is about impacting.

Unity will prove the doubters wrong.

Unity will prove the devil wrong because he is the father of lies and he hates togetherness.

Unity can gather people to
destroy or fix things,
    but please choose to fix rather
    than destroying.

As you get on with Life in school, at work, at home,
in church, in meetings, the gym, in a party or on media...
choose unity instead of division.

For the Lord says:

"Let us not give up meeting together, as some are in the habit of doing, but let us encourage one another — and all the more as you see the Day approaching."

Hebrews 10:25

The Lord also says:

"If we have been united with him like this in his death, we will certainly also be united with him in his resurrection."

Romans 6:5

In addition, The Lord says:

"May the God who gives endurance and encouragement give you a spirit of unity among yourselves as you follow Christ Jesus, so that with one heart and mouth you may glorify the God and Father of our Lord Jesus Christ."

Romans 15:5-6

Furthermore the Lord says:

"I appeal to you, brothers, in the name of our Lord Jesus Christ, that all of you agree with one another so that there may be no divisions among you and that you may be perfectly united in mind and thought."

1Corinthians 1:10

Finally, The Lord says:

"Be completely humble and gentle; be patient, bearing with one another in love. Make every effort to keep the unity of the Spirit through the bond of peace."

Ephesians 4:2-3

Think about this and try it out!

A human being normally has 5 fingers in each hand.

In life, in order to clap your hands, you need to unite your left and right hands together, so it can produce a sound, as you hit them together. That sound can be loud or not, depending on you.

Unite your hands and choose to make a loud sound through clapping in order to reach nations.

Now, when you put each 5 fingers together, what do you get?

10 fingers, right?

What do you see when you bring your two hands together?

A sign of prayer, right?

Once you clap, there's a sound. This means unity brings a sound. Because once you gather in unity, there must be a sound to effectively communicate.

Number 10 signifies completion, wholesome, efforts, positives, possibilities, opportunities and success. These elements are results of unity. When you are one there's no noughts. But when the noughts are added, it will become 10s, 100s, 1000s and millions.

This happens when we choose to unite our hands together. Meaning, you can't complete a project on your own, you need a team. 5+5=10 resulting into a team. 5+5= unity.

A sound brings communication, a signal, notification, awareness. Before coming into a room, for respect you can clap your hands. Clapping your hands is also a form of asking (Permission) or speaking out. Even in life, especially in Africa people clap their hands loud to know if the toilet is free or not.

In Genesis 1:28 The Lords says,
"God blessed them and said to them, be fruitful and multiply."

Unity brings prayers, enlargement, increase because the 10 can multiple into 100, then 1000, and a million.

Have you realised that when you clap your hands slowly, not much people will hear or notice you? This can't be unity.

But when you clap loud, everyone becomes alert, awakened and revived. A loud clap attracts many to hear. A clap births an echo. Those echoes can reach an ear. Your sound can unite, when an echo is formed, despite the distance. So, how loud do you want to clap, for a call to unity?